FIND YOUR WORK-LIFE BALANCE

Stop your work
from taking over your life

Written by Renée Francis

Translated by Emma Lunt

Coaching 50MINUTES.com

ACHIEVING WORK-LIFE BALANCE

- **Issue:** how can you stop your work life from impinging too much on your personal life? How can you find a good balance between the two, so as to be effective at work and relaxed at home?
- **Uses:** from the moment you enter the working world, you are confronted with the difficulty of finding a balance between your life at the office and your private life, particularly if you have a partner, children or an active social life. It is therefore useful to reflect on what makes for a well-rounded everyday life.
- **FAQs:**
  - Is it really in my best interest to have a clear separation between my personal and professional life?
  - How can I find this balance if I am self-employed or an entrepreneur?
  - What are the pitfalls to avoid in order to achieve a good life balance?
  - How can I start my day stress-free?
  - How can I limit interruptions, which cause wasted time?
  - How can I end my day feeling satisfied?

The issue of balance between career and personal life affects all working people, whether they are men or women; employees, CEOs, interns or freelancers; young or old; couples, single or divorced people; parents or not. It is not always easy to take on all the different roles that you need to play at the same time. Indeed, do you really leave your files behind you until tomorrow when you close the office door? Do you make yourself entirely available to your loved ones?

While it is normal to feel overwhelmed from time to time, particularly due to the accelerated pace of modern society, it is essential to find a stable balance that is in keeping with your aspirations regarding quality of life. Life passes by quickly; make sure you do not let it pass you by!

For this, there is no secret: it is a matter of refocusing on yourself and on what you really want, defining your professional and familial priorities, and organising yourself to give them the place they deserve. We are not talking here about agreeing to great sacrifices, but about agreeing to make choices and to undertake little adjustments. There is no secret, then, but there are some tips that can be useful to maintain balance in your daily life, manage your stress levels and optimise your time.

What is the best way of reconciling your professional and personal lives without hurting anybody, especially not yourself? How can you keep the fire inside you ablaze? These are the questions that this guide will answer.

WORK-LIFE BALANCE: THE BASICS

KNOW YOURSELF

It is impossible to find good balance if you do not know what is likely to push you over the edge. The first thing to do therefore involves taking a moment to reflect on what drives you to act in life and on your values, your driving force and your limits.

Prioritise your values

Advertisements, magazines, constant information, the internet, the difficulty of choosing (which stems from our consumer society), social, professional and familial pressure, etc. This is the scene surrounding us. It is difficult to know what we really want in this context! Yet this is the heart of the matter: determining what we need in order to be happy.

Do you know which values drive you to act? In order to get a clear idea of this, take a pencil and simply circle a figure between 1 and 6 (from most important to least important) in each line of the table below – but watch out, each figure can only be circled once. Forget all outside pressures and only consider what truly counts for you, in order to establish a mental hierarchy of these elements.

Other values can be added to those listed here, such as participating in a sports team, getting involved in a humanitarian project or association, discovering other cultures, etc. You should also be aware that the classification that you are going to obtain here is far from unchangeable. Our values develop over our lives: adjustments will be necessary over time in order to continually find balance.

Value	Importance in your value system					
Family	1	2	3	4	5	6
Work	1	2	3	4	5	6
Friends	1	2	3	4	5	6
Hobbies	1	2	3	4	5	6
Money	1	2	3	4	5	6
Relationship	1	2	3	4	5	6

Now redo this same exercise to indicate the positioning of your values in your current daily life. Which value takes up the most space?

Value	Current position in your hierarchy					
Family	1	2	3	4	5	6
Work	1	2	3	4	5	6
Friends	1	2	3	4	5	6
Hobbies	1	2	3	4	5	6
Money	1	2	3	4	5	6
Relationship	1	2	3	4	5	6

Now, compare each point in the first and second table. The first corresponds to the values which you should be prioritising to feel good. The second illustrates the place that these different areas currently occupy in your day to day life. If there are significant differences between the two, you are in an unbalanced situation, and you must use much more energy to keep moving forward. You must therefore put a strategy in place to reduce this gap as much as possible, or you risk falling apart.

To do this, the starting point is to identify what really drives you, your true motivation and the meaning that you want your life to have. This general meaning has already been hinted at through the responses you gave regarding your priorities.

Find your main source of energy

"What do you want to be when you grow up?". This is the question that we were all asked as children, and the question that we surprise ourselves by asking younger generations, as if our future job is the only thing that is likely to bring us happiness and fulfilment.

Take a step back: do you think that you have followed the path that you had imagined? Ask yourself this question, without limiting yourself to the professional side of your life. Use the values listed in the table above to quickly carry out a brief assessment of your life path. Have you made choices that are in keeping with your wants and abilities? If this is the case, then you are undoubtedly not far from discovering your driving force, the fundamental element that gives you the energy to move forward in the right direction and that makes you happy. All you have to do is find the common feature of your different life choices. Is it sharing? Commitment? Love? The need to understand? The desire to create?

If you are still searching for the driving force in your life, keep in mind that what you do every day does not necessarily define you! Maybe you are at odds with the values that you believe in and, consequently, your view of your motivation is undoubtedly obscured. It is up to you to focus on the values that you placed at the top of your list; these priorities that you set are part of your source of energy. Based on these, you will be able to find the ideal which you must reach for to find happiness.

Finding the meaning of your life will give you the confidence you need to feel more in harmony with yourself. Once your driving force has been identified, you will be able to rearrange your life so that it is not pushed back into second place. You will be able to give direction to everything you do as, unlike values whose importance varies constantly, your fundamental source of energy should not change.

Know your limits

Every individual has their own character, personality and temperament. These can be conditioned by the environment in which they develop. Professional pressure can sometimes lead some of us to go beyond our physical, psychological or moral limits.

In order to live a life that is in harmony with your values and abilities, it is absolutely crucial to clearly identify your own limits. Here we are talking, of course, about positive limits which are helpful and which allow us to respect ourselves, rather than negative limits which stop us from moving forward in the direction we have decided on, such as fear of being judged by others, shyness, the belief that we do not need anybody else, etc.

In this context, having limits is not at all pejorative. Recognising them means accepting that we are not perfect, which is a perfect approach! Imagine a world without limits: chaos would quickly prevail. We would do everything to excess and would not have the chance to bring out the complementarity of individuals. As for children, limits give them a degree of structure. We can understand our internal structure by identifying our own limits. Understanding the way we operate allows us to identify our strengths and weaknesses. It gives us a chance to maximise our assets and to personally express what does not fit with our field of activity or reflection.

We may also be led to overcome our limits. Sometimes we must be flexible, whether we want to or not. This involves making comprises and concessions. Even so, you must try to find a fair middle ground so as to not completely break away from the limits you have identified.

In the balance between your professional and personal life, you must assess three things. Answer the three questions below, without thinking for more than a few seconds. The answers must come spontaneously, and it is the first answer that counts.

- Do I spend too much time at work?
- Do I have enough time for myself and my loved ones?
- Do I often think about work during my free time?

OPEN YOUR EYES!

It may be that you do not think you spend too much time at work even though you are at the office for ten hours a day. Some people voluntarily choose to shut themselves away in their work to protect themselves from potential disappointment or simply to avoid getting emotionally involved in their personal life. If you are in such a situation, be aware that life outside work is the only thing you will have left when you are resting, on holiday, retired or if your company decides that they no longer require your services. Do you not want your personal life to be rich in emotion, relationships and challenges?

If you struggle to identify your limits, pay attention to the times when you balk at doing something. Is it due to laziness, lack of motivation, lack of interest, etc.? Or is it because the thing you are being asked to do goes beyond one of the limits that you have identified? Very often, this feeling of persistent unease that gnaws away at us is actually a limit that is trying to make itself known.

RESPECT YOUR NEEDS AT HOME AND AT WORK

Define your limits

Easier said than done! This is, however, one of the keys to success, as much in the world of work as in your personal life. Why is it sometimes so difficult for us to define our limits? There are two participants in this process: the person that sets the limits and the person that they are imposed upon (either themselves or others).

If you have trouble setting your limits, is it because you are not confident enough to express them? Are you scared of how they will be taken? The result, in any case, is that you do not express yourself. Or more precisely: you do not convey the message that you want to put across well. The question to ask yourself when you have difficulty putting your limits into words is this: what consequences could they have? Will they cause a conflict, uneasiness, some form of accountability or annoyance? Or will it be more a case of showing yourself in a more assertive way that you perhaps think that you will not be able to pull off?

Try to answer in a balanced way, aiming for a response which tallies with reality, without extrapolating or exaggerating. The only consequence of which you can be absolutely certain is that you will be the person who is impacted the most if you do not cut loose. Setting a limit is not destined to stop the world from turning, but to ensure that your own universe runs smoothly!

Managing to set your limits relies on improving your communication skills. It all depends on the way you present the outlines of what you can tolerate. Do not be afraid of being outspoken. Setting a limit also means freeing yourself from your own constraints. Assume your right to respect and do not hand this responsibility to a third party. Be capable of saying no without being aggressive towards the other person and without seeking external justification.

Everything is now a question of choice and circumstances. Indeed, for your own wellbeing and that of others, it is sometimes better to make a compromise which does not use much energy rather than entering into fruitless and never-ending discussions with the sole aim of complying with your principles. Ask yourself if it is worth fighting this battle and learn to save your energy for the things that are worthwhile. But beware: do not tolerate too many little things for the sake of avoiding conflicts. You will once again create an imbalance.

Put the importance of work into perspective

The working world has become so much more complex over the past few decades that it has at times become impersonal. Offices built from steel and glass which reflect the colour of the sky have no soul. The manager embodies authority to whom it is sometimes difficult to say no.

In order to find a good balance between your professional and personal lives, you must put things into perspective. Your colleagues and manager, amongst others, wake up every morning to go to work, while many of them undoubtedly have personal projects which they would prefer to concentrate on. Wanting to have a good quality of life and personal balance does not affect your ambition or motivation for your job at all, and you certainly should not feel ashamed. Just because we love what we do does not mean that we want to do it all the time or to have our thoughts taken over by our job! The best athletes need to take a step back to mentally prepare themselves for their best performances. Under no circumstance should we neglect the mental fatigue that builds up when we are working. It is the ability to put things into perspective that influences the way in which we face life with its joys and difficulties.

What do you do when you lack perspective, when you are caught up in a chain of events that seems out of your control? Many speak to their loved ones to discuss what is not working and to have a more detached outside view on an issue or problem, but often also to be reassured. In fact, the difficult situation of the world of work is a source of worry even for those who seem very sure of themselves. Internally, even the top manager faces doubts and stress. It is easier to put things into perspective when we know that we are not the only one in this situation.

TEST: HOW DO YOU IMAGINE YOUR DAY, YOUR WEEK, YOUR YEAR?

Everybody divides their time differently. In the same household, every family member will have their own view of time depending on their age and responsibilities. What is yours?

When we cannot put things into perspective, the idea of short-term is generally very present. You probably see your year divided into periods of work, punctuated with some holiday time here and there. From one week of holiday to another, you feel that you are holding your breath while waiting for the time to pass, without making the most of the rest of the year. We could compare this to watching a film in fast-forward in order to get directly to the funny moments without taking an interest in the rest of the story, even though it forms a series of constituent and significant events.

In order to get more out of every moment, try to mentally rearrange your time. For example, you could decide to establish a break, a time to stop during your week, in order to get a breath of fresh air. If you see the week as a block of five days ending with two days at the weekend, try to cut the week in two by planning, for example, an activity on Wednesday which you really enjoy. This interruption will energise you and will help you to overcome the little problems in the office so that they do not spill over into your personal life, because there you do not discuss work at all!

Stop feeling guilty

When we say imbalance, we mean unease. Indeed, in the case of imbalance, we very quickly feel that we have lost control. We do not feel on top of our game professionally or in our private life, or even both, which causes a feeling of guilt and worthlessness. We very quickly begin to compare ourselves to others and to only see the things that are not working for us or the things that we are not doing well. But in this era of social media and reality television, which give us the illusion of witnessing lives that are more thrilling and rewarding than our own, we must keep in mind that what we are shown does not always correspond to reality. Sometimes the most popular people are the ones that feel most alone, and you can be sure that even those who seem to have achieved everything with ease have to fight to maintain their life balance.

Get back to what is essential and stop comparing yourself to others. You can then enter into a dynamic of exchange, and you will have the chance to learn and interact with the people around you. On the contrary, if you are coveting something, are constantly comparing yourself or are jealous, you will only feed your illusions about the lives of others, without getting to know them. Yet it is not their lives that you should worry about; you must live your own life, completely as you wish.

You are not perfect? Even better. Perfection is deathly boring. Now that you know your limits, you can start taking steps to make up for them and make sure you form bonds with others (colleagues, family members, friends), while maintaining your independence, in order to overcome your potential shortcomings. Others can make your life easier.

Positive selfishness

In general, selfishness has a bad name. Known for being a trait of an excessive, or even abusive, personality, sometimes going so far as disregard or denial of others, the definitions of selfishness have given it extremely negative connotations. With society already tending towards individualism, it is important to go back to the ideas of sharing and solidarity.

Yet positive selfishness can find its place in this framework. How is it defined? It is the ability to not bend to the will of others and to not impede your nature and ambitions, without walking all over or ignoring those around you. Personal dreams and underlying aspirations are therefore brought back to the heart of existence. Thanks to a positively selfish approach to life, we can undoubtedly find joy by making the most of it, and re-establish a balance between our professional and personal lives. In other words, positive selfishness means, in practice, simply respecting yourself and earning the respect of others by respecting them.

This step stems from assertiveness, a non-violent communication method which involves expressing your own needs, without ever denying those of others, through listening and sincere conversation.

TOP TIPS

- Organise yourself in a realistic way: throw away the good resolutions that you cannot keep. Unattainable objectives contribute to a feeling of failure because they are too ambitious. Replace them with little daily tricks that do not require particular effort, but that make everyday life a little easier.
- Avoid fatigue by adopting a lifestyle and pace that are well-adapted to your needs. Opt for activities that are compatible with the amount of energy you have. Try as much as possible to plan these activities at times that will have the least impact on your physical shape. You will be less tired in the morning, which will enable you to begin the day more calmly.
- Prepare your things the night before. Rather than running all over the place in the morning, prepare what you will need to leave the house with peace of mind. This is even more important if you have children!
- Turn your phone off for two hours each night, especially if you are with your family or friends. Give them your full attention.
- Ask for help from your family or other people you are close to when you cannot manage everything you have to do alone. There is nothing wrong with asking for a helping hand. And if by chance things are not done your way, what does it matter as long as they are done?
- Work with those around you to find solutions. If you have children, for example, you could arrange with other parents to take turns doing the school run.

- Similarly, become a dream team with your partner by sharing the chores based on what each person prefers to do. A chore will always be a chore; nevertheless, if the chores are shared, you will feel like you have more time for yourself.
- Boost your efficiency at work to free up time for your family, time for yourself or time to spend at home. To do this, take an interest in time and priority management techniques. Make yourself a little plan for the day: divide it into several phases with a time limit for each task to be done. Cutting up your day is an effective method to not let it pass you by.
- Use the means at your disposal to help yourself in your daily life. Many technologies and applications have been developed with this goal in mind. For example, you can choose to do you grocery shopping online and have it delivered, or set up direct debits to cut down the time you spend on paperwork. Get yourself a smartphone that will enable you to check your emails on the go, but be careful not to abuse this when the day has ended. Make you sure let go of it after work!
- Buy a freezer, especially if you have children. Make bigger portions of food and freeze them. You can thus plan one or more calm evenings without having to spend time in the kitchen or having to go grocery shopping after work.
- Set your alarm two minutes earlier every day for a month. Get up immediately. After a month, you will have gained an hour in your day, without feeling any major difference: this time will be a chance to do some household chores that you will no longer have to do in the evening, to get to work earlier and thus leave earlier, to do some exercise

or to simply take time for breakfast.
- Look to the future, but without being absent from your present. We build our happiness today.

FAQS

IS IT REALLY IN MY BEST INTEREST TO HAVE A CLEAR SEPARATION BETWEEN MY PERSONAL AND PROFESSIONAL LIFE?

Yes! Leave your personal problems at home and your professional problems at the office! In this way, you give yourself the chance to think about something else in both environments. And being busy with other activities rather than dwelling on your worries is a source of inspiration to face them differently after leaving them to settle. This boosts reflection and encourages creative solutions. Clearly separating your professional and personal lives will therefore help you to remain focused at work and relaxed at home.

HOW CAN I FIND THIS BALANCE IF I AM SELF-EMPLOYED OR AN ENTREPRENEUR?

The weight on the shoulders of freelancers or entrepreneurs is different to that of an employee. A self-employed person does not always have the same schedules and their work often overflows into the weekends or evenings. The border between professional and private life can be less clear-cut than for employees.

Despite this, the ideal formula for reconciling your personal and professional lives also lies in giving yourself hours for working and others for your private life, without allowing the first to interfere with the second. As such, if you have offices/workshops in your home, it is better to clearly separate them from the rest of the house (at least visually, with a door, shutters, a screen, etc.), so that the professional life is not omnipresent, constantly reminding the freelancer of what they still have to do. You must accept that you will never have finished and be able to let go and breathe a little.

WHAT ARE THE PITFALLS TO AVOID IN ORDER TO ACHIEVE A GOOD LIFE BALANCE?

- Be careful with new technologies! An increasing number of people work outside of their office hours due to the presence of a work computer or phone that they take with them: as they are contactable at any moment, they feel forced to immediately respond to every external call. It is a trap that can be avoided by resolving to do without new technologies during certain time slots. Your personal time will be all the more protected as your mind will not be clouded by work. You must learn how to put the word "urgent" into perspective and be unavailable.
- Also, beware of the television and laptops. They tend to keep us awake beyond what is reasonable, thus running over into our hours of sleep that must not be neglected!
- If you plan on working part-time, be careful that you are not made to do five days' work in a shorter duration. Ensure this with your manager beforehand.

HOW CAN I START MY DAY STRESS-FREE?

When you wake up, concentrate on something that does you good: some meditation time to recentre yourself, a physical activity to refresh yourself, a household task that you will then not have to do in the evening, a good breakfast with your loved ones, etc. In this way, you will feel that you have had a satisfying day before it even begins!

Even if you are tired, avoid getting up at the last minute, as this forces you to rush around in the morning. As a consequence, when evening arrives you will certainly feel that you have been under pressure all day...

If, for one reason or another, you are still late, try not to let stress take over your day. Are you stuck in traffic driving your children to school? Perfect, this gives you the chance to make the most of being with them! Try to transform these potentially stressful moments into qualitative and positive moments.

HOW CAN I LIMIT INTERRUPTIONS, WHICH CAUSE WASTED TIME?

Interruptions, at the office as much as at home, can be numerous. Untimely phone calls, urgent intermediary tasks, people who come to ask you for things when you are very busy, etc. All of these things can make you lose precious time, which you could use for something more important.

It is possible to limit these sources of wasted time by planning times to disconnect, during which you focus on an important task without accepting phone calls, questions from colleagues, so-called urgent emails, etc. Organise yourself so that you are not disturbed by switching on your answering machine, closing your office door, putting on your headphones, deactivating notifications on your email server, etc.

HOW CAN I END MY DAY FEELING SATISFIED?

We feel satisfied with our day when we have achieved something. To do this, plan one important professional task each day which must be finished at the end of the day. The rest of your time must be organised around this priority task.

In terms of personal life, the idea is somewhat the same: we cannot be everything all at once, and each day has enough trouble of its own. Do not, therefore, try to cook a new recipe each day in the same week that you plan to do your big spring clean: plan your days reasonably and accomplish the tasks you have planned, nothing more. You will thus feel that you have both done what you wanted to do and that you have a little time to enjoy an invigorating activity (sport, reading, games with the children, etc.).

OVER TO YOU

MY ENERGY DRAINERS

In the table below, make detailed notes on the five time-consuming and energy-draining factors, at work or at home, that prevent you from having a good balance between your professional and personal lives. Then explain how you are currently handling the situation, which is clearly not enough. Finally, by reflecting on your resources and your personal assets, explore the possible solutions, which will enable you to find more energy or gain more time.

Energy-draining factor	Current management of the situation	Solution to try
Ex: I feel like I do not have time to do things at my own pace at work, as I feel under pressure. As I want my work to be done well, I feel unsatisfied and demotivated.	Ex: I tend to extend my hours and work more. I therefore spend less time on other activities, which also frustrates me.	Ex: I am lucky to have an extremely organised colleague, perhaps I can ask him for some tips on how to gain time on menial tasks, which will leave me more time to do important work well.

MY ENERGY BOOSTERS

Now that you have put your finger on some of the factors that are making your life more difficult, focus on the elements that give you energy and that help you stay on track, with the goal of leaving plenty of space for them in your timetable.

Every Sunday, if possible, broadly plan your week, by clearly splitting your professional and private lives. Write down only one important professional task per day and at least two of these invigorating activities each week. For the rest, organise yourself from day to day. Make sure to do this every week, no exceptions!

We want to hear from you!
Leave a comment on your online library
and share your favourite books on social media!

FURTHER READING

BIBLIOGRAPHY

- Gilbert, E. (2007) *Eat, Pray, Love: One Woman's Search for Everything Across Italy, India and Indonesia*. London: Riverhead Books.
- Lelord, F. (2002) *Hector and the Search for Happiness*. London: Penguin Books.
- McKenna, P. (2004) *Change Your Life in 7 Days*. London: Bantam Press.

ADDITIONAL SOURCES

- Fox, C. (2015) *Work/Life Symbiosis: The Model for Happiness and Balance*. London: LID Publishing.
- Dalai Lama and Cutler, H. C. (2005) *The Art of Happiness at Work*. London: Hodder Paperbacks.

Made in the USA
Monee, IL
07 July 2026